LONGHORN
on the Move

Written by Neil and Ting Morris
Illustrated by Anna Clarke
Historical advisor: Marion Wood

Evans Brothers Limited

Published by Evans Brothers Limited
2A Portman Mansions, Chiltern Street
London W1M 1LE

First published 1988

Printed in Hong Kong by Wing King Tong Co. Ltd.

ISBN 0 237 50971 7

INTRODUCTION

A new nation was born in 1783 when the Revolutionary War ended and the United States gained independence. At that time the western boundary was formed by the Mississippi River. Beyond that was a vast wilderness, the home of wild animals and nomadic tribes of Plains Indians.

In 1803 the United States made the Louisiana Purchase, buying over 2 million square kilometres of land from the French. For an agreed sum of 15 million dollars, this deal more than doubled the territory of the previous 17 states of the young republic. The new land stretched westwards from the Mississippi to the Rocky Mountains. Soon daring pioneers and fur trappers started forging trails into the forests, mountains and deserts of this unmapped new territory.

When Texas joined the United States, cowboys began driving huge herds of longhorn cattle northwards. The age of Wild West towns had arrived, and with it the rush for gold in California. This is the image of the American West that has lived on for over a hundred years, kept alive by legends and Hollywood westerns.

The cowboys' story had begun when the Spanish first landed on the shores of Mexico, bringing with them a herd of cattle. Mexican herdsmen later taught their skills to the first Texan cowboys, and the cattle grew strong and healthy on the plains of Texas. When the American Civil War ended in 1865, there was a great need for beef in the northern cities. And so began the long cattle drives to Kansas market towns such as Abilene and Dodge City.

This is the story of one young cowboy and his adventures on the long journey north. The information pages with the rifle border will tell you more about the life and work of the cowboys of the American West.

When Sam reached the ranch, he followed his nose. There was a smell of stew and he couldn't remember when he'd last had a hot meal. 'The name's Sam White,' the boy said. 'Where's the boss, I'm looking to sign on.' The cook knew the boy didn't stand a chance with Marshall, the new trail boss.

4

'We can't use kids on this drive. Get back to school,' Marshall
told Sam. 'When I could draw a horse and mark brands on
my slate, I knew I was too smart for school,' Sam replied.
'All right, let's see how good you are,' Marshall snapped.

Sam had trouble getting on the bucking bronco, but he
gripped tight with his legs and rolled with the horse. 'The
kid can stay with me,' Maclean said to Marshall.

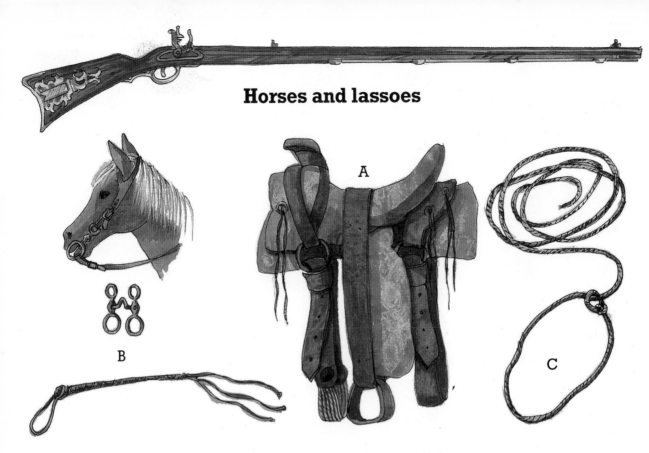

Horses and lassoes

A

B

C

Cow ponies were wild mustangs which had to be caught and tamed before they could be put to work. Bronco busters had the job of breaking them in. Cowboys changed horses several times a day. The horse wrangler looked after the herd of horses, which was called a remuda.

A) The saddle – the cowboy's most important possession.
B) Bridle, bit and whip.
C) Lariat or lasso.

The cowboy roped cattle and horses with his lariat or lasso, which hung loosely coiled from his saddle horn. To rope animals, the cowboy built a loop, whirled it in the air to keep it open and tossed it over the animal's head. He wrapped his end of the rope around his saddle horn. Apart from roping animals, the lasso was used to build a corral, pull wagons, haul firewood and hang cattle thieves.

Sam was up early next morning, ready to help with the round-up.
But Marshall had already left. When Sam rode out, he saw
a wisp of smoke and men with branding irons. One of them
waved his hat. Sam knew this was a warning to stay away.
Suddenly Sam recognized the rustler's face. It was Marshall.

'I must warn them back at the ranch,' Sam thought as he turned his horse. But who would believe a runaway kid? He would probably never make it anyway, with the rustlers after him. At that moment two riders appeared in the distance.

Shots rang out and Marshall and his men sped off. Sam was ready to go after them, but Maclean stopped him. 'Don't bother with that thief,' he said. 'I'll see he never heads a trail again.'

Branding longhorn

The Texas longhorn: long-legged and tough; average horn spread 1.30m to 1.50m; average weight 400kg.

Cattle first came to America from Spain. They were left to run loose over the plains of Mexico, California and Texas and developed into the Texas longhorn, the great cattle herd of the American West. After the Civil War, they were rounded up and driven north, where there was a great demand for beef. Their horns took many different shapes.

Each rancher had his own brand that marked his cattle. Because there were no fences, herds wandered for miles, and stray calves had to be branded and earmarked. Rustlers were cattle thieves, ruthless cowboys who took unbranded calves and put their own brand on them. They also stole older, branded cattle and changed the owner's brand with a cinch ring or a running iron. This was known as brand blotting.

1 branding iron; 2 cinch ring; 3 running iron.

Sam was treated like a regular cowhand. Maclean was the new trail boss, and he put Sam in charge of the horses. On the first day, the men drove the cattle as far as they could. Longhorn never liked leaving their home range.

Sam and the horses stayed with the wagon. Cook made a
hot stew, and at sundown the riders started coming in. But
it was hours before the longhorn settled down. Then at last
the cowboys could rest for the night.

Cowboy's equipment

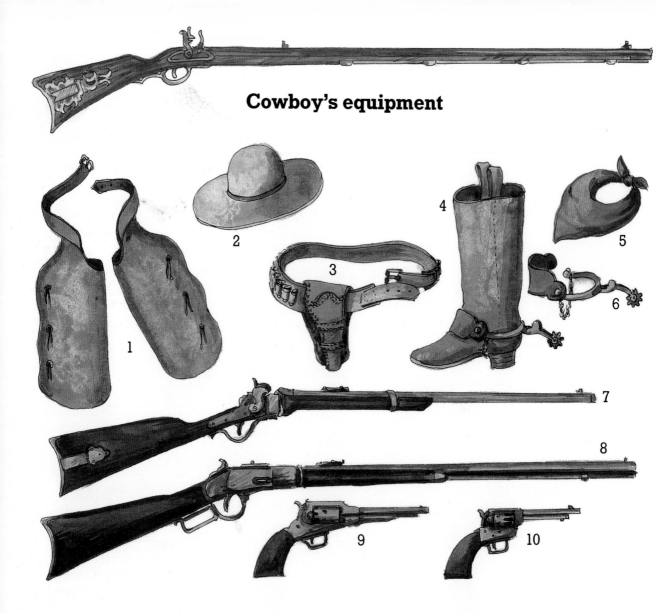

1 chaps, to protect his legs against scratches, rope burns and horns;
2 plains stetson; 3 belt and holster; 4 boots, with high heels to stop feet
slipping through stirrups; 5 neckerchief, to protect the neck from the sun;
in a dust storm it was worn over the nose and mouth; 6 spurs, to make the
horse speed up; 7 Sharps rifle; 8 Winchester rifle; 9 Remington revolver;
10 Colt 'Peacemaker'.

Day after day they travelled endless miles across the dry, barren land. There was little noise, as the ground seemed to swallow the trampling of the hooves. But the cattle were getting edgy. They needed water.

Then, for the first time in days, the cattle sensed they were near water. Suddenly the lead steer broke into a run. The cowboys rode hard to keep the cattle from going mad. Sam caught up with the steer just in time to pull him out of the quicksand.

'It's a poison lake!' Maclean yelled, as the longhorn
followed their leader towards the quicksand and the pool.
The cowboys fought the maddened animals away from the
poisoned water. But for some it was too late.

As they reached a river at last, the sky darkened. The cowboys feared a stampede. Lightning could sometimes set a whole herd off. They let the cattle drink as much as they could take.

But the cattle didn't want to cross the fast-flowing river. 'Show them the way,' Maclean shouted to Sam. At once he drove the horses in front of the longhorn.

The cattle followed the horses across the torrent. But they were scared, and half-way across they started milling around. There was chaotic shouting as the cowboys tried to break the jam.

On the trail

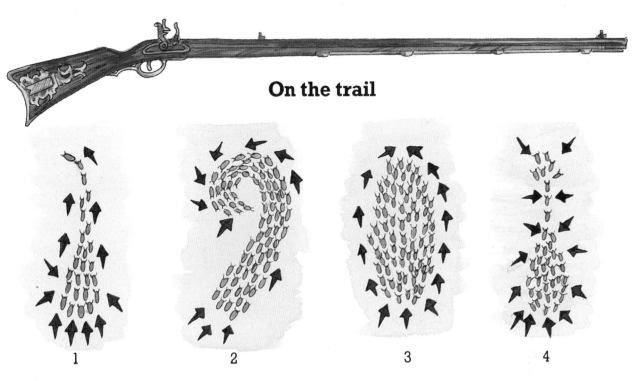

1   2   3   4

These diagrams show how the cowboys controlled a herd on the trail; the
arrows are the riders, who took up special positions to make the longhorn
do what they wanted them to.
1 Turning the herd to the left. 2 Stopping a stampede; the riders turned
the leaders to make the herd mill round in a circle. 3 Holding the herd still.
4 Counting the herd.

The cook was a most important member of the trail outfit. He was in charge
of the chuck wagon, which held all the food, cooking utensils and extra
supplies for the drive. It was an ordinary farm wagon with a box bolted on
the back. The cook's last job each night was to point the chuck wagon
towards the north, so that everyone knew which way to head in the
morning.

Sam never found out how the men broke the jam. No one said a word as they gulped down their coffee. They were exhausted. It was Sam's turn on night duty, but Maclean said, 'The kid needs rest.'

But Sam couldn't sleep. He listened to the night guard's song. Suddenly there was a shout and the sound of six-shooters. The cattle quickly got to their feet.

The earth trembled beneath the hooves of the thundering herd. A group of Indian warriors were driving off the cattle. Sam rode after them with the men, but suddenly a shot wounded his horse.

It took them till sunrise to round up the cattle. Then
Maclean followed the Indians to their camp. The trail boss
demanded to speak to their chief, and he soon found out
who was behind it all.

The Indians returned the stolen cattle and Marshall in
exchange for five longhorn. 'I should have known it was
you,' Maclean told Marshall. 'I'll see you get locked away at
the end of the trail.'

The cattle town

The trail ended at a cattle town. From there the cattle were taken by railroad to cities in the east. Stockyards, cattle pens and loading chutes were built beside the railroad. Cattle towns became wild places where the cowboys, after months on the trail, drank too much and got very rowdy. The townspeople hired a sheriff to keep law and order.

After three long months of heat and dust, it was good to see the town. Maclean handed Marshall over to the sheriff, and the herd was sold. Sam's pockets were full of money.

'You've done a good job,' Maclean said to Sam. 'Now have a little fun and a lot of sleep. You've earned them both!'

This map of the American West shows the trails the cowboys used to drive the longhorn North to the cattle towns.

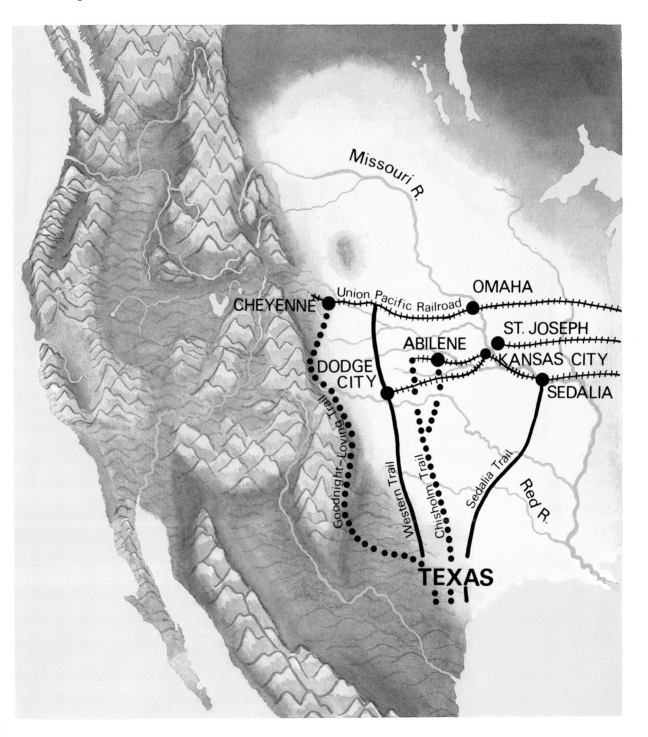